TABLATURE

THE HUGH MACLENNAN POETRY SERIES

Editors: Allan Hepburn and Carolyn Smart

TITLES IN THE SERIES

Tablature

Bruce Whiteman

McGill-Queen's University Press

Montreal & Kingston • London • Ithaca

© Bruce Whiteman 2015
ISBN 978-0-7735-4453-6 (paper)
ISBN 978-0-7735-8194-4 (ePDF)
ISBN 978-0-7735-8195-1 (ePUB)

Legal deposit first quarter 2015
Bibliothèque nationale du Québec

Printed in Canada on acid-free paper that is 100% ancient forest
free (100% post-consumer recycled), processed chlorine free

McGill-Queen's University Press acknowledges the support
of the Canada Council for the Arts for our publishing
program. We also acknowledge the financial support of the
Government of Canada through the Canada Book Fund
for our publishing activities.

Library and Archives Canada Cataloguing in Publication

Whiteman, Bruce, 1952–, author
    Tablature / Bruce Whiteman.

    (The Hugh MacLennan poetry series)
    Poems.
    Issued in print and electronic formats.
    ISBN 978-0-7735-4453-6 (pbk.). –
    ISBN 978-0-7735-8194-4 (ePDF). –
    ISBN 978-0-7735-8195-1 (ePUB)

    I. Title. II. Series: Hugh MacLennan poetry series

PS8595.H475T32 2015   C811'.54   C2014-906559-0
                                   C2014-906560-4

This book was typeset by Interscript in 9.5/13 New Baskerville.

In memory of Marion Jewell

CONTENTS

I
LANDSCAPES

ECLOGUE

Some souls are purgatorial by destiny.
D.H. Lawrence

The sheep crop ancient grass on hills
near Marshalltown, incontinent and dumb.
They slowly creep ahead, raising their eyes
as the need arises to gauge the changing sky
and keep a measured distance from one another.
Our car streams by a hundred yards away,
the babies gesturing at what they have no word for,
bleating in their own articulate babble.

Unprepossessing you might say the landscape is.
The highest hill around's a thousand feet,
and rubble is the order of the day
no matter where you look: it's fall and everywhere
the stubble of forgotten corn inters the feet
of foraging sheep. Even from a car you know
the air laments the heat of summer and loggy
flies whose very lives now seem a blessing.

The poet drives a Subaru and thinks of hamadryads,
flowing streams, and uncouth shepherds making
love in verse. What could be worse or further
from reality than lusting for Arcadia? It's almost
hell to feel imagination's off the mark
so laughingly beneath the tyranny of corn.
The sheep alone are patient, munching through
paradise lost or never thought of, sated

by the time the sun goes down and Venus
rises briefly in the sky, dim and low.
Amid the slow blandness of the coming
night, insane love lives on life support.
Exhaust fumes spreading across the fields
crinkle the noses of sheep and make us
crazy to get home, where love has a chance,
risky love, the love of last resort.

And the mute sheep stand unmoving now,
thinking it no shame that we race by
at unimaginable speed. The pastoral
in the rear-view mirror blinks out fast.
The automatic headlights coming at us
wink and stare, climbing and falling on
the gently rolling hills. Our babies
sputter into soundless sleep.

REGRET

Nothing penetrates mind
like the yellow sun, and quells
regret. Pure light falls

everywhere, on pine trees
and the late fall squirrels
fat with premonition. It

warms their necks and
picks out flecks of
interstitial shadows in the

grass that modulate
and blink, on and off
the earth. The mind

as well turns off and on
with autumn's unaccustomed
shine, its bric-a-brac and

deep distractions nothing
in the perfect light of
day. When cloud

occludes the sun then
memory stirs and
whirrs the kernel

of some lasting hurt
like a dying leaf
twirling towards earth.

Already dead it
needs to glint one final
sunny red or yellow time.

ALMOST NOVEMBER, IOWA

We've lost the cats to
winter habits. They eat and
sleep invisibly, coverted in
cupboards where they put on
weight and wait out
spring's far cry.

Leaves race by the
windows, insane to get
nowhere fast. The fence
corrals them all at length,
holding them fast in
heaps. Humping lovers

need heat too, now as
never before. They find time
unpromiscuously for
each other, exerting – what? –
life in the face of
the almost coming dark.

THE UNMASKING

Every dance imagined
by the most nimble
body is a bergamask,

limbs akimbo, the
mind three steps
behind, as usual

lost on the cambered earth
where invisible music
demands we caper to

survive. The grand
impassioned dance of words
that lumber on the

whiting grass, lurching
now one way and
now another, makes

a choreography of snow.
And the bird in his
remote and homely wisdom

sees ungainly marks
beneath his perch
and silently departs.

FIRST SNOW, LAST STRAW

Cars have vanished out of doors, and
women wrap themselves in deep red wool.

Our sense of community drifts like snow
against a door. The colour of the sky has changed

and no one will be coming out for months.
A contest of wills goes on in the absence of flowers.

It's strange to think how leaf and calyx make life
worth getting up for. The piano itself

seems incapable of making music, Brahms
or any other incontrovertibly winter composer.

A wedge of trumpeter swans flying south
overhead makes all the music anyone will hear

until spring. Who doesn't want to see the grass
again, if the world doesn't come to an end first.

BEING POSSIBLE

… if being possible depended on anything other than Destiny.
Fernando Pessoa, *The Book of Disquiet*

Winter is acrid and one day at a time.
Somewhere out of harm's way the crows

huddle to keep warm, and no fierce
disinclination to sensual life makes

any difference at all. The cold
is persistent like air or fate.

It seems the sun is gone for good,
its epic engineering faltering at last.

The crows then launch themselves
aloft, fated to repeat their

limited leap at rapture again
and again, and not to rue

the pleasure that they miss
in blissful possibility, heart-felt

need.

BEING POSSIBLE II

Cuatro pájaros sin rumbo
en el alto chopo están.

                    Lorca

A sudden gust of wind and
a dozen birds collapse as one,

struck by some ancient lust
to flee a shaggy pine

and perch elsewhere, as though
they owned all trees.

Nothing ghastly in a crow's
dark past bespeaks its end.

Nothing's aimless in its fated
flight from one branch to the next,

as white snow dribbling to the
ground falls past a crow's black

eye, unmoving as the night.

LOREM IPSUM

For Ken

Poetry is made of words that mean nothing
without music. The language
is a given. I am not happy.

Happiness is intrinsic only to the
unexamined life. The snow piles up
and the birds ignore the feeder hung

expressly for them. You can't provoke poetry
or the future. You can only substitute
what happens for what you expected, what

you longed for. The blue jay blithely
flies by spilled seed as though it were
spring, and food everywhere for the taking.

A MIND LIKE A PACK OF SCATTERED CARDS

The measured intrusions in the snow
of squirrel tracks and rabbit tracks
leave humans nothing daunted,

who make holes the size of tractor tires,
flailing clumsily to drive a dog away
and monumentalizing failure.

It snows again and everything disappears.
The cardinal scatters red from tree to
tree, contingency of nothing so much as

arctic air from Canada or mushy fate or
poetry – the way words suddenly occur
to a mind set free from need and grand intent,

the masquerade of I. Joyous
birdsong out the studio window measures
passing time, inflecting everything that's

heard. A painted lattice on the garage wall
is blank, awaiting April's colours, earthy
garden muck, sweet woodruff and chives

that thrive as winter wanes and dies.
Dumb weather, intransigent heart, mind
that can't make sense of anything but

words – words, like tracks in the snow, with
a lovely life of their own. Like a palindrome,
the day looks every which way the same.

THE ROCK THAT LOOKS LIKE A BEAR

The water encroaches on it,
sculpting the form from a

blank stone slate: a nacreous
animal with a kerchief

behind its ear. She lies
perfectly still as the river

flows slowly by in its
relentless permanent embrace.

High water, low water, she is
drowned or sinks into

indefiniteness by turns. No
love can save her

no matter how it endures.

THE SKUNK ON THE BRIDGE OVER
THE GIHON RIVER

He waddles a car-length
ahead of me in a light rain.

It's wet and almost dark, skunk-
weather, skunk-time. A

male, I bet: that swagger.
I stagger behind him slightly

drunk, composed enough to
keep away. Supposedly he'll

stamp and hiss before the
final *vade me retro* of

stink. I think the test
is mine, not his. His

twin stripes lit by incandescent
light now lead the way.

Skunk-god and river-god under
a godless sky keep

drunkards holy and safe.
He descends into a hole

in the lawn, needy himself
to sink without a trace.

SPRING SNOW, VERMONT

It's April, and the snow
drifts heavily to the ground,
clotted and quickly turned
to wet. The air alone is
white. Sight despairs

and the heart too. This is
no way for spring to start.
The river that flows
from paradise swells
with muddy stuff,

rushes hard and
flecked with white heads
west to Lake Champlain.
It's dusk. The sun must
be in the west too, sullen

and invisible, like a
broken heart. It's dead
easy to "have a mind of
winter" when the heart is
also white. The snow will not

let up. It surrenders
to the stream, a disappearing
dream of spring. Everything
reverts to snow, the
heart and all we, shivering, know.

TRANCES OF THOUGHT

The pallid grey sky gives way to
shiny signs of spring that linger for
weeks. Squeezed between seasons,

death retreats again, a little less far
this time, marred by sunlight
only minutes older than yesterday,

pandered to by fervent squirrels
alert to any change in the wind.
The disconnected birdbath lying

on a choppy sea of last fall's brittle
leaves will get another chance.
It's a minor human presence

in the garden the birds own, the way
they own the sky. They'll condescend
to slosh. The world slops in spring.

Spring's messy and stirs up thoughts
of everything's okay and saved from
doom – the kids on pogo sticks

next door, leaping clumsily at heaven,
the death-obsessed squirrels instantly
querying each quick move before they

make it, buds on the trees. Outside
the trance of every day's magic spell –
the insect sting of knowing death's

around the corner – there's nothing
tragic in a bird's grey wing,
not even in its certain disappearance.

OBJECTS ON A DESK

I

A Cenozoic ammonite to start with.
It probably lived not far from here

in the Pierre Shale, fluttering its
fleshy body now turned to stone in

what was once a sea, now turned to
stone as well. I'm far too petrified of

death in twenty years to think of *millions*.
It takes my breath away. Death, that is.

II

Ceramic labia in celadon blue, a
hexagon in shape, and true to the real

woman if you think about it, deltas of
Venus notwithstanding. The foam of

hair caught perfectly in waves and cues,
a symmetrical frame around the point

where pleasure starts and radiates
like a star, hot in four dimensions.

III

The pyrite cluster glistens in the sun,
a crystal with seeming eyes that cannot

see for all their bright intensity.
No one's really taken in by things

that represent themselves as other than
they are. It's quintessentially human to

pretend. Our clastic hearts defend deception.
Only a fool would say otherwise.

IMPROVISATION ON A LINE OF HÖLDERLIN

Voll Verdienst, doch dichterlisch, wohnet der Mensch auf dieser Erde.

The scudding clouds of arriving summer
pull overhead. Balanced in
windowpanes, so unlike the

static art we make of them,
images of everything alive outdoors
revolve and shimmer and are

renewed. Every moment birthday cells
evolve in muck and come in time to be
the flitting bird, or bird that's giving

chase. The least trace of a firefly –
we watch them, sitting close at dusk
on the grey back steps – batters the heart

with something approaching happiness.
To live poetically is to honour
the skein of it all: the tam-tam of

dripping water from an eave,
leaves burgeoning through a
prism of colour, impossibly

desirable flesh, words and their
resolutely human music. The rivers
flooding with the melt of snow

threaten summer and the life we
make in it, as though nothing
were sure or crafted to last forever.

In this sense God, as Hölderlin
might have said, wears shorts
and will not let himself be caught

dead by the camera's click. We thrive
because He is sick of the world.
The clouds drive lovely overhead.

The world goes on as people die away. Even the
brutest of the brute persist in eating
and the replication of their kind as though nothing had

ever happened. The sun comes up and pours its yellow
light on all that matters: intricate ménage of the blue-grey
house and all my loved ones who live inside it.

The sun's most welcome grace transforms the
untranscendent little earth of children who die
and grownups who do not wither and do not care;

fair enough. No one owes his faith to perfect
strangers, or so it seems. The restless flit
of money and the lust for things are easier

to countenance. The scrutable sun invests it
all, death and triste imperfection of spirit, so as
almost to make us disbelieve its generosity.

Grieve and celebrate and worry for the young,
whose lovely hearts can little think of anything
but love, love and their peerless spot on earth.

The stone and wooden house enfolds them like a
womb, blue on an afternoon of dreamless sleep.
Time creeps on beneath a glowing winter sun.

HISTORY

Goethe traveled in Africa in '26 disguised as Gide and saw
everything.

Tomas Tranströmer

Impermanent trees that line the streets
breed green illusions. Love rains hard
from dark grey skies. It comes and goes.
Everything ecstatically comes and goes:

Canada geese that seem to have no
innate sense of north and south,
winter and its tragic husbandry, the
body's heat, poetry's delirious squawk.

Fools with nothing in their ghastly heads
talk endlessly of what the past can teach
as though it weren't all out of reach, even
what the heart has learned. Rank

invention is as much a part of us
as TV news or whom we confide our
deepest fears to. Imagining a table
or a browning yard of rutting deer

confirms we live as passionately as
Gide in Congo watching recrudescent
hell, missing nothing. He wrote it down
and changed the way the world works.

The ease with which we picture streets
devoid of trees, or Brahms on his
deathbed, sallow and drinking Rhine wine
from a crystal goblet, long past music,

means more than all the battered cars
and failed machinery bailed for shameful
passage overseas, or even our carefully
curated private histories – life as far back

as the human heart recalls.

II
LOVE POEMS AND OTHERS

AND TO LIVE WITHOUT A PLAN
(A LOVE POEM)

… et nulla vivere consilio
Propertius 1.1.6

The ruckus of lyric poetry, Propertius knew,
comes down to this: life sucks and fuck

the long term. Let's live without a plan.
Your cunt illuminates the dark as much or

more than Christ's stark moralistic rants. He
came not to send peace, but a sword. What

word is worse and likely more to drive us
back to bed? Consider the birds.

They cluck and fret but instantly forget
what ill fate befell them in the hunt for food

and sex. Darling, it's one way to make things
work, the classic shrug. Turn out the light

and hug me. History sinks the unplanned life,
I know. I know it's just a fantasy to think

we're allied with concupiscent birds or
could be. But love me fiercely like we were.

When lips touch, much
as the gentle rain gently
touches down to earth,
distinctions disappear.
The ground grows lovely
and wet, some secret chemistry
exerts its law and two
are one. An old saw, that
keen desire. No one
wants to stay himself
for long. Dive headfirst
into the other, that's the
direst human need and
prick to song. Wetness
always radically is a part
of it, wetness and indistinctness.
I want to be you, you see,
not me, or not me alone.
Me alone is the enemy.

NULLUS AMOR TANTI EST

Cynic Ovid got it wrong.
Hard-nosed love is always worth
the vivid pain. Get

me out of here's a waste
of time, you're stuck
for good. Fuck with hope, with

need, with amorous
expectation all you want,
lover mine, heart's ease

never dies the death of
fear or loses faith.
Hang on as though your life

depended on it.
Readjust your sense of
heaven. Heaven is here and this.

OBSESSIONS

Not a hint of sun today.
The sky is the colour
of the garage roof, its

grey-born shingles now in
shadow. The roof is cocked
designedly at 45 degrees. The

trees mock its pointed regularity
growing any which way they
like. Sixteen crimson

leaves remain on the
Japanese maple as though
hung by a lover to catch one's

eye. One by one they
click and fall off into the
dense red thatch below.

Love is stowed there mute for
months to come. Out the
stile, back of the big back

yard, small trucks lumber by
laden with salt, headed
somewhere in the craven cold.

A crow desists for lack of
heart or crass old age
and plummets to the lawn,

murderous crow, crow that
used to be a lover, guardian
angel of the heterodox.

Three days on, a mass of
fleshless feathers sits
amid the grass. Crushed

bones too abide, naught else.
The sky is the colour
of crow feathers now despised.

INVASIVE PROCEDURES

How inaccessible the heart is
to an untrained hand.
Autonomic love can fail at

any time, but won't if we
don't give up. Each time
you lie with your back

to me I am deeply moved,
the mere fact of getting prone
a seeming miracle of sorts.

I dream the stupidest things,
the painful singing death of
Alexander Scriabin for one,

lying there in the bare
arithmetic of sleep beside
you, or the silent falling

down of every tree in sight.
Death and still destruction.
Ancient fears again take up their

prehensile hold on my heart,
breaking the skin to
renew their deathless stake.

SCHEHERAZADE GARGLED

The drops of milk
that spill onto the
table from your
breasts arrest the

moment more than
all the lights dissolving
in a snowstorm in
gloomiest Iowa. The

boys have wakened
silently from sleep
and need to slake their
thirst. Your nipples

know it first and we
catch up. The body's
coarse command is
always bright and more

demanding no matter
what we think or
consecrate in art or
intimate desire.

THE MIDDLE OF A LIFE

It is all tragedy and cows.
  Ken Norris, "The Middle"

No sudden spectral hallucinations
compromise its earthy certainties:

heavy snow and baby pee and too little
sleep. Sex is no longer a tutelary

god but planned, like dinner.
The prospect of Mexican take-out

terrorizes our week. None of the
local joints is a winner.

Chronic back pain makes a poet
cranky, and it's hard to read a

novel: there's little time for that.
The Year of the Death of Ricardo Reis

took three long months, and Poe's *Eureka*,
whatever it is, is like the dishes:

once a day for twenty minutes.
The *Register* gets more attention.

But then the *Dona nobis pacem* of
Bach's B-minor Mass comes on the radio

and changes everything. The babies
prick their ears and Kelly smiles.

There's nothing bovine in the day's devotions,
ever. Never disbelieve the flesh or

weather even at their tragic worst.
Love imbricates everything we, loving, do.

DEEP SNOW PECULIAR HEART

The red jeep sits abandoned in the
snow, its mud-flaps hanging by a thread.
Bitter weather inches it towards

junk. Its broken windows let in light and air,
slight recompense for being dumped
there in the yard. Nothing will save it now from

innocent neglect. The point of things
is that they die and no one cares.
There'll always be more things, jeeps

and other creepy encumbrances
on the heart, to crack and waste away
in abnegation. Stained with

flecks of paint and brown debris,
the snow recovers its imperishable
whiteness in the longer term,

lasting out beyond the loving care of
hearts or sad abuse of unremitting
stuff.

GREY DAY, DEATH IS FAR AWAY

A rusty birdbath overturned in snow
is all among the wreckage of the day
that stays indelible. Whiteness crawls

inside the bowl where heaps of
convoluted sparrows once
turned rainy water brown

with antic exercise. The birds
swim elsewhere now or not at all,
frantic like all of us for spring

and its watery rescue. Love needs
to be reinvented, Rimbaud said, in his
despair at ever finding it, his

longing for paradise. It must have felt
like nothing could entice love back,
glare of sunny day or bit of luck,

rare green lawn or likelihood of heaven.
The prairie grass spikes upward
through the snow and barely

registers the fitful wind.

THE WARNING

After Robert Creeley

For love, I'd throw my
aging body off a bridge,
naked, and swim to shore
with algae in my eyes –

love, I mean, for love
demands some stark surprise,
lest its virtue fade to little
more than dumb intent.

FEBRUARY 15TH

A glaucous SUV drives by and
like a weary baseball player spits high

water that's new on the street
today. A gibbous moon is up.

Empty branches seen against a
cloudy sky are just themselves,

like love or loneliness or fading
light. Nothing that matters is out of sight

but you, and you are here to stay.
The snow is melting as I watch.

I'm not concerned. I'm even hopeful.
Love says green grass lurks anew out there.

Ken's in Thailand defying winter,
absorbing a thousand smells and filling
pink notebooks with well-wrought poems

about middle age, about the stink
of life in America, about love and rage.
The phalaenopsis in a Bangkok market

attracts his eye, and like a girl
undressing, a poem starts to blossom in his
head. *Phom yag roo jak khun,*

he thinks, I want to get to know you,
poem and girl and beautiful pink
flower at the floating market of Taling Chan.

The forced enjambment of a dream
throws disparate elements of memory
and who-knows-what *ensemble*

and a story gets told, like poetry,
that's full of wonder. No logic in that
strange collusion of female blood and

fishy sport, and man standing beside his
word. No need for it, when flowers and
girls and the thousand metamorphoses

of dreaming confiscate the thinking
brain. Again another notebook fills up,
like rain inside the flower's cup.

RAIN ON THE WINDOW

It drips like paint and savages the view,
turning a simple strung wire into
an ECG. What you see

out the window is always a measure of the
heart in any case – wisdom, lore, the
vivid recall of dreams, imagination's

mounting evidence that trees, for one,
are infinite beings. They seize the earth
and slowly take on heaven like an army of

prickly angels bent on love's victories.
Crows mass on their woody limbs
and caw in praise of weather, no matter

what. Do birds feed in the rain? A blurry
finch finds the hanging seed sock too wet
for excavation and hurries back to his

perch in the leafless maple tree.
The rain continues falling. The heart
feels gloomy for no especial reason,

gleaning hints of worse to come from
tints in the glass reflected out of passing
shadows, watery light, life's flit.

THE WORDSWORTH THEFTS

The catechumen watches snow descend
in March upon *the common range
of visible things* and blanches like the

snow itself. It's risible to think that
anyone alone in small-town USA
matters anyway no matter what the

weather, or wreckage wrought upon
the very heart of man by love or
thunderstorm or shaken curtain of

spring snow. We all know this is
how it is. It's being null and void
that helps to make us love one

another, and *poets connected in a
mighty scheme of truth* attest
that Nature doesn't give a damn: at best

they're all a dumb misunderstanding,
our desires. We think and feel,
compose poems of epiphanic grace,

erotic shelter, and game passionate feints
to make the human world more real.
These our *own pursuits and animal*

activities are everything and nothing,
equals of the sun one day and
gone the next like fallen snow or

sex, but finally *genuine knowledge
fraught with peace.* Hot days lie
ahead that cannot last.

POEM INCORPORATING A FRAGMENT
OF IBYCUS

No flock of cranes but commoner birds
enhance the sky. It's spring, it's Iowa

and feckless grackles dominate the yard,
flinging seed everywhere, reckless and

self-absorbed. Like a hundred minor suns
the daffodils have run their course

from green to yellow in a single day.
Crocuses and bluebells spot the maculate

grass while Laconian girls who show their
thighs walk ignorantly by and disappear like

unselfconscious animals. It's what they are.
Unpredictable desire drifts on the spring wind

and painful shifts in the heart occur like
sudden modulations in a score by Schubert –

the F-minor Fantasie for four hands the mind
obsessively intones, that recrudescence

of unrequited love or sorrow for love requited
and undone. An intelligent wasp

interrogates the soffit's flaking paint,
thinks better of his chance to arrogate

a bit of the human world beneath his feet
and disappears suddenly over the high roof

of the house. Love goes too, or stays, like wasps
and birds, obeying love's instinctual law.

THE SORROW OF INACHUS

sed nocet esse deum
  Ovid, *Metamorphoses* I, 662

The tearful god in confinement longs
only for death and cannot have it.
His naked body does not waste for
lack of food and drink, or passionate
arousal by another's flesh. He cannot
taste a thing or bear the woven mesh of
any garment on his limbs. There's
only one emotion left to him. It's

vast. The cracked unfixable world
speaks hard of loss and he engages
with it, planning to vanish too, knowing
he cannot defy his undying heart but
harbouring hope for sly annulment
of the laws of keeping faith. Hopeless
and feeling only grim suppression of
all sensual enjoy, he must endure.

A god's old privilege does not keep him
safe or sure of happiness. Death punishes
by its unavailability, leaving the
eternal body gazing out a window
at the rain, with nothing more to say.
Pain falls and does not stop. It mars
the shadow of every visible thing, a
cold and watery encumbrance on the world.

ARCHILOCHUS UNWITTINGLY EXCHANGES
A COW FOR POETRY

Inspiration ex nihilo, a sixth sense for the
heart which cannot make do with fewer:

fragrant narcissus in a spring garden, Reger's Variations
and Fugue on a Theme of Bach, cut sweet apples,

the emerging yellow sun, a yearning hand laid on a
yearning cheek. We have such lovely infinite moments

every day and die for their continuance.
The barefoot man who treads the cold wet

grass, pulling a wagon and a child who laughs,
hearing the passionate morning squawk of birds,

pauses to set some brush alight and
tends ecstatically to the mounting flames

which flare, then sputter and go out. He'll soon
be thinking about his lunch, about his

hunch to bring some daffodils into the house
for their colour and scent, about the death of

bin Laden, which only when the radio's turned on
over beer will he hear of. The fire in the grass will

haunt his dreams tonight despite its seeming
ordinariness. Like Archilochus' cow it's gone now,

but everything depends upon the memory of it
in a single beautiful dreamer's head.

BEYOND RECOGNITION LOST IN LOVE

The lovely rain falls in sheets of
translucent paper, hard as pepper,
ticking in the tin gutters and

dribbling in runnels down the
petals of silent flowers, drubbed into
life after weeks of dreary sunshine.

Their colour brightens even as they daggle
and sag toward the greening grass.
Two cats, listlessly staring out a

grubby window, barely give the pinks a
glance. Their bleary eyes cannot see the way
the flowers dance and light up the afternoon.

In the rain, what chance is there for
love? Birds are solemn and off the wing,
unmoving on some rainy roof or branch;

the wet world is unnervingly still.
Love will try to raise itself in love's
rangy way, in its passionate need for

careful obliteration. We love to
die to ourselves for good feeling and
spiritual practice. It's as holy and

domestic as the weather. The body of
your lover fills the naked room like rain,
a room of no volume, no distance, no

slant, and there's scant room for pain or
ambiguity. Bodies that burn for each
other are what compose the liquid day.

COME WHAT COME WOULD

Upon one of the Kingsmill islands, then, I determined to plant my
foot, come what come would.

Herman Melville, *Mardi and a Voyage Thither*, ch. 3

The rumpled man who tunes the
plangent Steinway inches his way
into the empyrean. Soon he will stop

and start again and head the other
way, ordered notes repeating multiple
times, betraying a hertz or two of difference

only, as he pulls on a pin. The rise is almost
inaudible.
              The heart's like that, moved
by tiny achievable harmonies,

open and attuned to anything, begging
not for surprise so much as for
blessed reassurance. It's only lies

it doesn't suffer well, stray hurt,
deliberate target, rhetoric that puts it
out of kilter. What's despondency but a

clamorous music in the air,
baffling the heart's desire to be keen
for what's to come, beat by passionate

beat. Glamorous love can push a pin into
glamorous love for no apparent reason,
deflating hope and devastating eden.

HELEN

The imagination spans beyond despair.
                                    Hart Crane

The hanging feeder casts a shadow like a
leaping fish, fading black against a
solid wall, out of time in the

high wind. It dangles in a lull but
no bird comes. The birds are anywhere
but in the air right now, caught in a

moment of the earth's sure turning
out of history, content to wait it out.
And some ridiculous chemical in the

brain, straining to bridge a gap in
what connects the weather and the mind,
brings Helen up and all the dreary panoply

of desire and despair. Where does the
notion of a beautiful girl and the
waste she trails behind her naked back

progressing through the gusting world
and our imagination of her find an end?
She brings more dark consideration

of how things almost got to be
without her, lovely her head hung in
mute agreement with the scariest thought

of all: the death of love. Winter
threatens once again and all the heart's
pristine despair. That's it: despair is

never done no matter what imagination's
consolation, no matter what love flies in the face
of this is the way it was.

WHITE RAIN IN A BLACK SKY

Nothing is visible on a moonless night
when thunderstorms annul all light

except their own brief focused interruptions
in the sky. So the rain is white

in front of countless lightning strikes.
It falls on itself noisily in garden ruts,

where rotting squash and unchanging green
tomatoes drip invisible drops in perfect time.

Countless heartbeats race at thunderclaps
and fantasize relentless doom, savage

aftermath with rain that's red and light
that won't recur, a permanent dark.

Can love's enduring spark be snuffed?
Is it white rain in a temporary storm?

MAKING LOVE AT 10 P.M.

The automatic floodlight over the garage
blinked on hours ago. The babies are asleep.

We're tired but it's date night. The sheets
are cold and we could be forgiven for

choosing sleep. Heaven knows we need it.
Almost everything is dim and quiet. The cats

doze somewhere else and can't disturb us
as fitfully they do when we're in bed.

I hate the dark but put out one last light
and slide beside you, flinching so as

not to make you shiver at my touch,
waiting for our couple heat to rise

and make us one. For pillow talk our
list is pretty grim, but soon the flesh

exerts itself and instinct floods the bed
like light. Knowing their way, my fingers

set out on your lovely body, determined
to correct the ordinary hours that we

fall through day by day, and make us one.

III
MUSIC AT THE HEART

THREE MINUTES OF ECSTASY
WITH ARNOLD SCHOENBERG

How mere notes on a staff
make happiness remains
harder to fathom than a

lover's kiss. Why did she
say yes (the cello line!), then
no, bliss over like a

gunshot or a perfect
five-one close. Three minutes
before the end and I am

ravished, taken out of my
ignorant stony self by the
sounds (music is love, say

it), then cast adrift in
silence. Silence
hurts more than harsh words.

Love is music, or at least
it ends, no matter
what degree of bliss.

No one sees it coming,
though we know its human
pedigree. It can't go on

forever, or won't.
The cello fades to triple p
and disappears in air.

THE SILENCE OF AN AFTERNOON OF MUSIC

By 4 o'clock the sun
is barely lighting on
the trees, all beyond

sight now more than
half the time. Far out of
earshot the birds

decry the end of day
and any thought of
seeing through the air.

It's darkening as the
crows take flight and music
roils in the mind.

Hours till darkness
but night reigns early
on the snow, as low

in the sky the sable
crows deploy a score
that vanishes at once.

No barren misappropriation
of the fading winter light,
their transient music

is a quartet of Fauré,
once started set
to play out in the ears

and heart and not to
stop. Imagination's perfect
replication of those

scattered spots of dark on
white goes humming
in the wordless afternoon.

THE BLUE PIANO

I cannot bring a world quite round,
Although I patch it as I can.
                        Wallace Stevens

In the afternoon air the music is blue,
a sonata of Scarlatti as melancholy

as a leafless tree, scarred with snow
and catatonic against an unmoving sky.

Gone grief, so why does music speak
the triste elaborations of a lifeless day?

Maria Magdalena Barbara breathed hard
and played these notes that linger

in the room like words that cannot be
retracted, their palpable bruise

unseen as though inflicted
by a skilful torturing god.

Harmony's lure and the
sage cryptography of song

inure us to the tragic
truth of music's always being

blue at heart. It merely
comes and goes and no degree of

rage or long diminuendo
convinces us it lasts. Or only

long enough to break our hearts.

POLYPHONIC SETTING FOR WHITE

Snow falls hard in the morning air as a
fugue by Haydn fills the room, and one by
one a white poinsettia drops its shriveled

leaves. The tiny tick they make
at falling briefly turns the heads of sleeping
cats, who shake it off and stretch and

fall asleep again. *Dux* and *comes*
come and go, while sleet is blown against
the window-glass with metronomic clicks,

eliding outside and in. Haydn's grim
interrogation of his subjects *sotto voce*
struggles to be heard. The snow in canon

fuses all directions, and time stops dead.
The cats breathe hard and dream perhaps
of Mallarmé's magic water-lily, closed and

white, white as the viola's plangent theme.
Nothing, it seems, is whiter than imagination's
disembodied things.

THE YSAŸE SONATAS

The leaves turn over in the wind and
gleam in the weakened sunshine of early
March. They seem real enough to me,

like the sturdy larch at the end of the yard.
Music starts up on the radio. It's
Ysaÿe again, sounding like a flock of

sparrows and finches fighting over
seed spilt from a feeder. Such
sublime music from a single violin

blots out birdsong from outside,
the true inharmonious melodies of spring.
It's too soon anyway for spring

to come. The birds should know, their
brawn is all the more on show
with more snow coming in the days ahead.

It's all an abyss, thought Baudelaire,
the things we do, the things we long for,
language, dreams elaborated in sleep.

The tempting cynicism of a dying poet –
that cultivated hysteria – counsels
disregard for the intimacies we love

and live by, music heard at any
sweet time of day, "birds in the trees,"
Ysaÿe's double-stopped harmonies.

Music, as Baudelaire confessed,
is the sea that rocks despair
to sleep, out of the reach of

thought's intense contaminations.
It easily imagines bird and wind, fraught
emotion and incandescent need.

Ysaÿe picks thistles off his corduroy
pants and plants another seed.
An old violin leans against a tree.

LUTE MUSIC

Yeats said music makes us crazy.
At its behest, lazy distracted men
and women fall into swamps or drown

embracing the moon. Oh but that was booze,
the test that Li Po failed, flailing
visibly in silence, out of air and

out of time. No grace there but in the
poetry, the story of his life. Poets
choose to live or die by music, says

the muse from out of nowhere.

BERCEUSE

I want you breathless
on my faithful arm.
It holds you loving
where you lie in pleasure's
sly redoubt, away from
harm and all the trying

awful contrarieties
of life, the sometimes
lurid strife of getting through
the day. Consoling sex and
after-lull, shallow and full
of fleeting dreams, waking to

the babies' cries. It's okay
now. They cry in hunger
only and that's good. They'll
soon be back to sleep, and we
in deathless memory of
briefest love, will find sleep too.

A JOYFUL NOISE

J'écris. Et la campagne est sonore de joie.
Francis Jammes

Everything lasts. The rain falls hard and
fills the house with typing noise, as though
the thunderstorm were madly poised

to write the works of Shakespeare
in a random hail of words and letters.
The daylit world is fraught

with incomprehensible poetry
wrought from baby babble and
blushing lovers knowledgeable

only in the after-glow of what they
said or tried unblushingly to say
with loosened inarticulate tongues.

Everything lasts. Outside, the bourdon
the rain makes in the grass and
maple trees swells and recedes.

The flowers chitter. The plash of sticks
descending from an antique oak
irregularly drowns them out, pitter

and soak. The wind increases from a
whisper to a roar, inspiring
ecstasy in the roses and clematis

which flail at heaven like lovers
coming to the end of love. There is
no end of love. Everything lasts.

TUMULT

The crows have congregated in the street
and caw at every passing living thing.
They do not love, despite their

universal scorn and seeming lack of
self-restraint. It isn't fair
to ask intolerant birds and other

lolloping creatures to act like us.
They don't have faith or long for
something more than weather –

string quartets and unsought kisses
and one more book, just one more book
from Marianne Moore. "All this fiddle,"

indeed. How raucous they are, for god's sake,
overpowering thought and focusing
the lovely moment, rough music while it lasts.

FAREWELL TO STROMNESS

The sudden end of innocence makes us weep.
Dark elaborate dreams of absent suns
and creepy greying days without

respite. Crows massing
silently in tree-tops, restless and
insolent somehow, even out of ear-shot.

Tears cannot fall fast enough
to keep up with a brain score
of passing trains and babbling homeless

men who've lost their will for
sex and life. The trauma of the
everyday's imbued in every

truculent cloud that runs before the
icy wind. Their bruising faces
scurry by and scare the life

below to death. Caustic
rain draws motley dying leaves
to fall in hecatombs, transient

pyres, menhirs built and blown away
in seconds. How radiant hope seems
and how easy to give it up for good.

Lying on a stained and dirty couch
a woman overhears the piano and
stanches tears with random stabs

at her unraveling sleeve. The intimate
apocalypse underscores the simple
and distressing tune enveloping her.

Somewhere up the snowy line a handsome
animal has caught its leg in a trap

and died. The early sun imposes
on the morning gloom and shines

against its glassy eyes like stars
falling in a winter sky. Lumpy

fishermen bring home rainbow trout
and put them in the deep freeze for

Candlemas. It's hard to imagine the
sex life of birds. Their cries

interrogate the trees at any time of day.
Music takes over the morning air, a

string quartet by Schumann, instigating
breath, polymorphous and perversely

playful. The air is fading blue as the
light emitting diodes in a million

electronic devices begin to disappear.
Scenting death, the necrophilic crows

arrive by twos and threes. There has to
be a radiant happy ending somewhere.

ACKNOWLEDGMENTS AND NOTES

I am grateful to the editors of the following periodicals, where some of these poems have appeared previously: *ABZ: A Poetry Magazine, Briar Cliff Quarterly, The Fiddlehead, Literary Review of Canada, North American Review, Poetry Quebec,* and *Wapsipinicon Almanac.*

I want to say a deeply felt thank-you to the central characters in the rescue opera that was my life in the summer of 2013: to George Fetherling (orchestra director), to Neil Flowers (répétiteur), to Milt Jewell (principal bass), to Ken Norris (librettist), to Theo and Severin Whiteman Maynard (silent but loving partners), to Brenda Whiteman and Lynda Simpkins (principal sopranos), to Jesse David and Thera Emily Whiteman (grown-up children's chorus), and to Bill Zachs (principal tenor). I would never have made it without all of you.

Ken Norris pushed me back into the conventions of the line, and my gratitude goes out to him. The Vermont Studio Center gave me a month's time to make the transition back. George Fetherling read the manuscript and offered crucial advice and assistance. My editor, Allan Hepburn, offered some suggestions for revision which made *Tablature* a better book by far.

A few of the titles of my poems have been borrowed from other writers (and one composer), and I wish to acknowledge my petty thefts: Friedrich von Schiller ("This Kiss to the Entire World"), Ovid ("Nullus Amor Tanti Est"), Ralph Gustafson ("Scheherazade Gargled"), John Keats ("A Mind Like a Pack of Scattered Cards"), Peter Maxwell Davies ("Farewell to Stromness"), and Edgar Allan Poe ("The Last Spot of Earth's Orb"). Most other allusions and borrowings are obvious or explained in the texts, but a few further notes may save curious readers some trouble.

"Being Possible II": The quotation from Lorca's poem, "Canciòn de Novembre y Abril," in Alan S. Trueblood's translation, runs "Four aimless birds / are on the tall aspen."

"Lorem Ipsum": This is a bit of untranslatable Latin that comes from a passage in Cicero that became standard to exemplify typefaces in specimen books and sample text settings.

"Improvisation on a Line of Hölderlin": The line quoted from Hölderlin comes from a poem with no title that begins "In lovely blue," and has been translated thus by Richard Sieburth: "Well deserving, yet poetically, Man dwells on this Earth."

The epigraph to "And to Live without a Plan," from Propertius, is translated by the title of the poem.

"History": The Tranströmer epigraph is from "About History" in *The Great Enigma: New Collected Poems*, trans. Robin Fulton (New York: New Directions, 2006).

"Nullus Amor Tanti Est": The title of this poem is from Ovid, *Amores* II, 5, 1. Peter Green translates the proposition as "No love is worth *that* much."

The italicized fragments in "The Wordsworth Thefts" are all from *The Prelude*.

"The Sorrow of Inachus": The epigraph, "sed nocet esse deum," has been translated by Allen Mandelbaum as "sad fate indeed / to be a god." Inachus was a river god whose daughter, Io, was raped by Jove and afterwards turned into a heifer, leaving Inachus eternally disconsolate at her loss. The full story is told by Ovid in *Metamorphoses* I.

"Three Minutes of Ecstasy with Arnold Schoenberg": With the phrase "Three minutes / before the end" I had in mind the overwhelmingly beautiful concluding bars of Schoenberg's String Quartet no. 1, op. 7.

"The Ysaÿe Sonatas": Eugène Ysaÿe, the Belgian violinist and composer, wrote six sonatas for unaccompanied violin.

"A Joyful Noise": The line from Francis Jammes' poem means "I write. And the countryside resounds with joy."